Happy Endings

Wendy Craig

Happy Endings

Stories Old and New

Illustrated by Gillian Chapman

A DRAGON BOOK

GRANADA
London Toronto Sydney New York

Published by Granada Publishing Limited in 1982

ISBN 0 583 30519 9 paperback
ISBN 0 246 11786 9 hardback

First published by Hutchinson Junior Book Ltd in 1972

Granada Publishing Limited
Frogmore, St Albans, Herts AL2 2NF
and
36 Golden Square, London, W1R 4AH
866 United Nations Plaza, New York, NY 10017, USA
117 York Street, Sydney, NSW 2000, Australia
100 Skyway Avenue, Rexdale, Ontario M9W 3A6, Canada
61 Beach Road, Auckland, New Zealand

Printed and bound in Great Britain
by Cox & Wyman Ltd, Reading
Set in Times

Acknowledgements

The following traditional stories *Ewungelema, When the Water Disappeared* and *The Jester who Fooled a King* have appeared on the Music for Pleasure record *In Front of the Children*, read by Wendy Craig, and manufactured by EMI records.

Dedication

To Julia and Charlotte

Contents

Edward Albert

Edward Albert twiddled his ears and gave a loud snort. He was able to twiddle his ears because he was a hippopotamus and ear-twiddling is something they can do which we can't. He was snorting because he was upset. He had just trodden on a porcupine's paw by mistake and made him cry. Edward Albert was a very soft-hearted hippo, but clumsy and awkward. He was a friendly soul and he couldn't bear to hurt anyone or anything, but because he was rather large and exceedingly heavy it was almost impossible for him not to tread on something. He sat down on the end of his tail with a thud and had a little think.

'I'm probably sitting on something now,' he mused sadly. 'A beetle or two perhaps, or an unfortunate worm. I expect I've squashed them; really it's too sad, I can hardly bear it.' Two large hippo tears, about half a pint each, welled up in his eyes and began to descend his lumpy cheeks. He lumbered to his feet, and hardly daring to look, peered at where his bottom had been to survey what damage he'd done, but it was a nice smooth bare patch and he'd squashed nothing. 'Oh, thank goodness,' he gulped. 'Perhaps if I'm very careful indeed I shall avoid hurting any more friends.' So he set off home on his tip-toes looking very carefully at the ground before he put each foot down.

His sisters, Susan and Yvonne Hippo, were playing a game of hop-scotch in the yard. Susan was just going to throw her stone at number four when she saw Edward Albert out of the corner of her eye and grabbing Yvonne she bursts into shrieks of hysterical laughter. He was tripping along on the very tips of his toes with a happy smile on his lips and his ears twirling like small windmills. He was so happy because he hadn't stood on a single creature since he worked out his plan; not even a centipede, a flea or an ant.

'Honestly, Edward Albert, you do look peculiar, are you feeling all right?' asked Susan.

Yvonne sniggered.

'No, I'm not,' said Edward Albert, a bit down-in-the-mouth. 'I'm trying not to trample on things because it hurts them. I'm always going to walk on my tip-toes when I'm outside in future.' And he daintily toed his way across the yard. His sisters stifled their guffaws and went on with their game. They were very fond of their brother but they thought he was being a bit silly and he'd soon grow tired of balancing his big fat body on the tips of his stumpy feet.

Next day was Sunday, and the whole family, dressed in their finest, set off for church. Mother and Father in front, children behind. The girls were wearing flowery bonnets and Edward Albert sported a new checked cap, a present from his Auntie Mary. He lagged behind the others a little because he didn't want them to notice that he was tip-toeing, but his mother happened to glance round and saw him.

'Come along, Edward Albert, don't be slow darling or we shall be late. Why are you walking in that peculiar way?'

Edward blushed a bright pink and looked at the ground. He shuffled about a bit and waited until his mother had caught up with father before he set off again. It was just the same all the way home. The girls giggled and teased him and his father thought he was being quite ridiculous, but mother didn't say anything, she waited until they were back in the house, and while she was shelling peas for lunch she had a little talk with him.

'Darling, why are you walking on your tip-toes these days? I've noticed it from the window but I haven't said anything in case you wanted to tell me yourself. Are your feet sore or something? Have you got a verruca?'

'No, mother,' he said quietly. 'You see, I don't like trampling on things and squashing them. I've hurt so many of my friends the insects and I've decided to tread very carefully in future.'

'You have such a sweet nature, darling,' said his mother, popping a couple of peas in his mouth, 'but you know, it isn't always possible not to hurt things. I understand how you feel, but people will laugh at you and make fun of you if you dance around on your toes all day long. You must be prepared for that.'

'I don't care what people think,' said Edward Albert.

For the next month or so, Edward Albert carried out his plan. He became very good at it, rather like a dancer. He could trip along quite quickly, he could hop on one foot, he could glide along as though he were on skates, or leap in the air and change feet before landing.

Of course, the villagers did laugh at him and torment him at first, but after a while they got used to it and began to admire his prowess. After all it's not every hippo who can dance about as lightly as a feather avoiding tiny insects on the ground. He became a great favourite and used to perform at festivals with the village band, raising loud cheers of admiration for his sprightly capering.

One day, Edward Albert's mother sat down at the kitchen table and, taking out her lined note-paper and fountain pen, she carefully wrote a letter:

Dear Mr Ringmaster,

I've heard that your circus is coming to our village next week. I should like to draw your attention to my son, Edward Albert. He's an exceedingly talented dancer and I feel he would have a most successful career on the stage.

Yours sincerely,
Marigold Hippo

The whole family was on tenterhooks, waiting for Edward Albert to have his audition. He practised his pirouettes and *entrechats* every day, and taught Yvonne and Susan a marvellous *pas de trois* to the music of 'Colonel Bogey'. As a finale he threw them both in the air and caught them gracefully, one on each foreleg.

As had been expected, the ringmaster was beside himself with excitement when he saw Edward dance, and he pulled a contract from his inside pocket and waved it enthusiastically in Father Hippo's face.

Everything was signed and sealed and Edward's 'first night' was approaching fast. He was to make his debut at a Saturday matinée. His mother had made him a beautiful suit – red satin trousers and a royal blue bolero trimmed with sequins. He had taken a bath, polished his toe nails, and rehearsed every day for several hours until his performance was quite perfect.

As the moment drew near, however, Edward began to feel extremely nervous. He paced up and down outside the big tent, listening to the children shrieking with excitement as the acrobats performed their terrifying feats. He was next on the bill, and he was shaking and quaking with stage fright. The clowns tried to reassure him, patting him on the rump and telling him jokes to jolly him up, but Edward's legs felt shaky and his heart seemed to be thumping in his mouth. Suddenly he heard the trumpets blare out the fanfare and the ring master announced him in a loud voice. He wanted to turn and run away, but the clowns pushed him into the ring where he felt himself blinded by the spotlights and deafened by the roars of delight from the audience. He stood trembling for a few seconds as his music began.

'Oh golly,' he gulped. 'I can't dance – I know I can't! I can't stand on my toes, my legs feel so

wobbly.' The audience fell silent. The music fumbled to a halt, and Edward dropped his head in shame. Suddenly, his eyes focused on a small line of ants marching doggedly across the sawdust of the ring.

Without hesitation Edward, as though lifted on strings, rose on to the tips of his toes and in order to avoid trampling on them, tripped across into the centre of the arena. The conductor raised his baton, the band began the music for the second time, and as though inspired, Edward Albert danced as he had never danced before. It was a triumph! The audience clapped and cheered. They threw flowers and chocolates and bags of crisps into the ring as a tribute to his performance, and made him return seven times to bow to them. 'Hippo-hippo hurray' they yelled.

Well, that was the beginning of it all. Edward Albert became the most famous hippo in the world, a dancer of great distinction. The Nureyev of Hippos. He married Dora, a charming hippo fortune-teller and together they travelled the world in a caravan painted with stars.

The Jester who Fooled a King

An Old Story from Poland

A very long time ago, Poland was ruled by a king called Jan. He had a splendid court, lots of courtiers, servants, and ladies-in-waiting, and he had a jester called Matenko. Now a jester is what we would call today, a comedian, somebody who makes everyone around him laugh. A jester would tell funny stories, turn somersaults, do tricks and keep all the visitors amused. He wore brightly-coloured clothes and he had a cap with bells.

Matenko had been a great favourite for many years with the King's household, but unfortunately he was now very old, and his wits were not as sharp as they had been, and he wasn't so funny, and people didn't laugh at him much any more. The Lords and Ladies yawned when his told his jokes. They'd heard them all before. They said that he was a bore, and they told the King it was time he got rid of him. But the King was very fond of him and felt sad about it. He didn't really want to get rid of his old friend, but what could he do? A jester who doesn't make people laugh isn't really a jester. So one day he put his arm around the old clown's shoulders and said: 'Matenko, my dear old friend, the time has come for you to retire. I will give you a little cottage in the village and a few gold crowns, for we haven't much money I'm afraid – the last state ball left us almost bankrupt – you and your wife can go and live your old years in peace.'

Matenko was heartbroken, he had enjoyed his life at court so much. He loved the glitter, the comings and goings of the visitors. He loved the great banquets and feasts. He loved being the centre of attention.

He and his wife packed their belongings and walked sadly and silently down to the little cottage.

It wasn't very long before the poor old couple were penniless, and, of course, Matenko couldn't get another job because all he knew about was being a jester. They were very hungry and very worried, and racked their brains as to what they should do to earn money for food.

One night Matenko had an idea. He sat up in bed and tapped his wife on the shoulder. 'Are you awake Elzunear my dear?' he said.

'Yes, Matenko. What is it? Are you all right?'

'Yes. I've had a very good idea. Tomorrow you must go to the Queen and tell her that I am dying. No, no, that I have died, and that you are penniless and left all on your own and you don't know how you are going to live.'

'Oh, what a splendid idea. Oh husband, you are clever,' said Elzunear.

So the next morning they got up and the old lady

dressed herself in her poorest rags and laughing said, 'I suppose I ought to look sad if you are supposed to be dead.'

'Well, hold some onions near your eyes,' said Matenko, 'and you'll look as if you have been crying for hours.'

'Oh yes, that's a splendid idea, that's exactly what I shall do.' She went out into the little garden and pulled up a couple of onions and sliced them. My goodness, they did make her eyes water.

By the time she arrived at the palace, holding the onion to her eyes every few steps, she looked as if she had been crying for months and months.

She knelt down before the Queen and pretended to sob. Really it looked exceedingly convincing with the onion tears pouring down her face.

'Oh Queen, have mercy on me,' she said. 'My dear husband the jester who made you laugh so many times, has died and I am left alone, friendless, with no children to support me and no money, and I don't know what I am going to do, I may starve to death.'

The Queen, who had always liked Elzunear, felt sad for her and asked one of her ladies-in-waiting to hand her a purse. She took a little bag of golden coins and gave them to Elzunear and said: 'Poor woman, here take these coins. Give your husband a decent funeral and see that you have enough food and warm clothes to keep you until you join him in heaven.'

'Oh thank you, thank you, you are such a good Queen,' said the old lady, bowing her way out.

She almost ran all the way home. What a

wonderful trick it had been. Old Matenko was terribly pleased with her. She had done it so well.

'It's easy, it's easy. It's too bad you can't die every day,' she said, laughing and kissing her old husband.

'Now,' said Matenko, 'I think it would be a good idea if you died and I'll go to the King.'

'Oh, do you think we ought to?' said the old lady.

'Why not, I worked for him for fifty years. Surely he can keep me in my old age.'

So the following day the old clown cut up some onions, held them to his eyes and made his way to the Palace. Soon he was brought before the King.

He walked across to the great throne and knelt down, his old bones creaking. 'Oh your Highness, Gracious Majesty; my dear wife has flown up to heaven and I am left alone, penniless, with no one to look after me. Please help me for I'm a feeble old man.'

The King had always loved Matenko and he drew a big purse full of coins from his pouch and gave it to him saying: 'Dear Matenko, it's lovely to see you again. Here take this money, see your wife has a decent funeral, and get some good soul from the village to come to your cottage and cook you a meal each day and clean your house.'

'Oh, Your Majesty,' said the sly old clown. 'You arc good and kind, may God bless you.' And he creaked his way out of the throne room and then galloped on his old shanks back to the cottage.

'Look, look Elzunear, look what I have got, enough for us to live comfortably for the rest of our lives. How fortunate and how clever we are.'

They skipped around their little kitchen table

throwing the coins in the air and shrieking with glee. Then suddenly Matenko thought a very serious thought – if the Queen and King talked to each other about what had happened they would realize that they had been cheated and of course he was quite right.

At the palace the most terrible argument was going on.

'Matenko is dead,' said the Queen. 'And he has left a poor widow.'

'Nonsense,' said the King. 'It's Elzunear who is dead and she has left the poor jester.'

'Well,' said the Queen, 'Elzunear was here yesterday and she said that it was Matenko who was dead.'

'Rubbish,' said the King. 'I have only just left Matenko . . .' And so it went on . . . and on . . . and on.

Finally the carriage was ordered and the royal party set off down to the village to find out exactly who was dead.

The old clown saw them coming down the hill and said to his wife, 'Quickly, we must both pretend to be dead . . . come along.'

'Dead! we don't look as if we're dead!'

'Put some flour on your face.'

'Flour on my face? Whatever do I want with flour on my face?'

'It will make you look white as though you're dead.'

They powdered each other's faces with flour and lay down on the bed and pulled a sheet over themselves, having lit a candle at each corner of the bed, and they lay there trying not to laugh.

There was a fanfare of trumpets, the King and Queen had arrived outside their little house. Matenko and Elzunear lay under the sheet shaking with giggles . . .

'For heaven's sake stop laughing,' said Matenko. 'Try to look as though you are dead.'

'I'll stop laughing when you stop laughing,' said Elzunear. 'You're making me shake all my flour off. Oh stop it for goodness sake.'

The King and Queen entered the little cottage and looked sadly at the bed.

'Our dear old friends,' said the Queen. 'I wonder which of them died first.'

'Well actually I did,' said Matenko, sitting up.

'Lie down you old fool,' shrieked his wife, whacking him on the head with a pillow.

'You villain,' said the King. 'You tricked me. Get up at once and tell me what you mean by this disgraceful behaviour.'

Matenko rose from the bed looking very ashamed, his white floury face all little runnels with tears of laughter. 'I'm awfully sorry, your Majesty, we really didn't have any money left because you didn't give me very much when you sacked me, so, well yes, we did play a trick on you to get some more.'

A tiny snigger escaped from the Queen. The King clapped his hand over his mouth, but out came a great guffaw, and the courtiers, seeing the King laughing, all burst out laughing too.

'Why Matenko,' roared the King, 'that's the funniest joke you've ever played. Come back to the palace and be our jester again. I never realized how much I missed you.'

So they all set off, back up the hill together, laughing all the way.

Alaster Mouse and the Boring Princess

Princess Stupenda raised a haughty hand and waved her servants away. Life was a bore: she was beautiful, she was rich, and she was extremely unpleasant. She'd spent the morning having her hair curled, painting her nails and trying on dresses, and now there seemed nothing else for Stupenda to do except sit and stare out of the window at the beautiful palace garden which seemed to her as boring as the rest of her surroundings.

She was just fifteen but she didn't care to behave like a child any more. She regarded running about playing hide and seek or tag as unladylike and not at all the way a princess should behave. On the other hand, she didn't feel herself to be grown up yet, and conversing with courtiers or attending balls and other social functions bored her until she could have fallen asleep, or fainted, or disgraced herself by screaming at the top of her voice, 'Help . . . I'm bored!'

She stared out of the window with a scowling face, thinking nasty thoughts.

Now little did she know, but Alaster Mouse was sitting in his hole in her bedroom skirting-board peering out with beady eyes at her dressing-table. He was transfixed by a bottle of bright red nail polish that Stupenda used to paint her toe- and finger-nails. It fascinated him. It was so bright and jammy, and Alaster Mouse longed to paint something with the brush on the end of the screw top.

Everything was quiet, the princess was scowling out of the window in the next room and there was no one around. Alaster Mouse plucked up his courage and crept out of his hole. He twiddled his whiskers and shuddered with delight at the thought of the thick red goo. What a temptation! It only took him a few seconds to clamber up the gilded leg of the dressing-table and then . . . oh joy . . . the bottle was his. He clutched the top with his soft pink paws and twisted. It was quite difficult, he had to do quite a bit of huffing and puffing and he felt rather hot and bothered when finally the cap was unscrewed. The brush tipped, and a thick red blob of varnish settled gently on the glass top of the dressing-table.

'Diddle-de-dee, Diddle-de-dee,' sang Alaster Mouse. 'Now for some fun.'

First he tried painting his nails and flashing them about like the princess, then he decided to draw pictures on the mirror. He drew a flower or two, an aeroplane and then a cat. It was quite realistic and frightened him a bit, especially with red varnish dripping from its mouth. 'Like mouse's blood' he thought, and rubbed it out with a tissue. Then he had an idea and wrote in large letters 'Prinsess Stewpenda is a boar.' His spelling was atrocious. He scampered down the dressing-table leg and into his hole, leaving bright red blobs all the way behind him.

Stupenda stretched, yawned and gave a groan. She rose on her satin-slippered feet and crossed to her bedroom, a cloud of perfume wafting from her beautifully arranged hair.

'I suppose I shall have to get ready for lunch,' she muttered angrily. 'The Ambassador from Nestapife is coming, oh how boring. Hello? . . .' She stopped in her tracks and gazed in horror at her dressing-table. Red nail varnish was spread everywhere, and there, right across the mirror were the words 'Prinsess Stewpenda is a boar' in the most awful spelling and writing. She was furious and rang the bell angrily for her servants.

'Such insolence,' she screamed. 'Whoever did this will be severely reprimanded. In fact he will have to leave my service. I have never been so insulted! never! The Prime Minister shall be informed, the Brigade of Guards called out if necessary to rid us of this impudent wretch.'

Alaster Mouse tittered in his hole and admired his scarlet nails.

They finally calmed her down and prepared her for the luncheon, and as she was descending the great marble staircase of the palace, a tiny smile played round the corners of her mouth. 'Ha, with all this excitement,' she thought, 'I haven't felt bored for at least half an hour.'

The next day, Princess Stupenda was lying on her chaise-longue fanning herself, feeling quite desperately bored.

Alaster Mouse's whiskers were twitching and his eyes were shining with excitement. Stupenda's private maid had left her lipstick in a silver case on the dressing-table.

'What a lovely big red crayon' he said, pulling off the top and smearing it in a circle of vermillion around the bottom of a jar of cream. 'I think I'll do some patterns,' he whispered. 'Diddle-de-dee, Diddle-de-dee.' He did a row of dots, a row of zig-zags and then two rows of very nice loops. After that he had a couple of games of noughts and crosses, and then he wrote across the mirror 'Prinsess Stewpenda is a stewpid boar', stuck the lipstick in a pot of cold cream, and slithered bumpity-bump down the leg of the gold-painted dressing-table, and into his hole.

Stupenda had decided to count her jewels in order to stave off her boredom, but the sight that greeted her as she flounced across towards her dressing-table made her heart leap with anger. 'How dare they? How dare they?' she kept asking herself, wiping up the mess with cotton wool and a damp face flannel. She didn't call the servants this time, she was afraid they might laugh behind her back and she had a very nasty feeling that the message on the mirror was true. Perhaps she was boring people more than they were boring her. She sat on the edge of the bed and had a long think about this. Meanwhile, Alaster Mouse was trying to lick the lipstick from his whiskers. He decided it was definitely raspberry flavoured.

The following evening Alaster Mouse was to be seen quietly prising open a box of eyelashes left on

the princess' dressing-table. 'Diddle-de-dee, Diddle-de-dee'. He coated them with glue and stuck them on his top lip like a moustache. Then he took a big, fluffy powder puff and dabbed it around his nose. His face was as white as a pastry board. He caught sight of himself in the mirror and nearly split his sides laughing.

The princess entered her bedroom in a swirl of satin and ostrich feathers, looking very beautiful, ready for a State Ball. She heard someone laughing and stared with round amazed eyes at the little mouse with false eyelashes stuck on for a moustache and white powder all over his nose, capering about pulling faces at himself in the mirror. Then she watched fascinated as he picked up an eyebrow pencil and wrote 'Prinsess Stewpenda is a big fat boar'.

'So!' she said, as her slender white hand closed over the small furry body, 'It's you who've been writing rude things about me. You naughty little mouse. How dare you?'

Alaster Mouse was unafraid, he twiddled his moustache to try to make her smile, and blew a cloud of powder in her face. 'I thought it was time someone let you know how boring you are. Yes, you're boring because you're always bored. It must be making you very miserable. Try taking an interest in other people for a change instead of always thinking of yourself, you'll be surprised how interesting they are, and you won't feel bored any more.'

Stupenda knew in her heart that he was right and popped him gently back into his hole.

After that she tried very hard to listen to other people, understand them, help them, and laugh with them. And like magic she seldom felt bored again and she became known as the most interesting princess alive.

She bought Alaster Mouse a nice set of paints and a thick white block of paper to use when he felt he needed a bit of fun. It was not that she minded too much about her make-up, but she felt she owed him a present for being the only one who had dared to tell her what a bore she was.

When the Water Disappeared

An Old Australian Story

Long ago in Australia lived a huge bull-frog and he had the most tremendous thirst. He simply couldn't stop drinking. He lapped up all the lakes and he swallowed down all the streams, and quite soon the whole land was completely dry and all the animals and birds and fish were parched and dried up, with their fur dropping out and their tongues lolling about and their eyes bulging. The little fish were flopping about in the mud at the bottom of the dried up pools.

The bull-frog had grown bigger and bigger because he was so full of water, he looked as if he was going to burst. He was so greedy that his mouth was full to the brim and he had to keep it tight shut otherwise the water would have come gushing out. He was disgusting.

Now the animals were very, very worried about the situation and they called a meeting.

'What are we going to do?' they said. 'Because if we don't do something we're going to die of thirst.'

'I know,' said the wombat, 'let's have a concert and then we'll get all the animals to be as funny as they can to try to make the bull-frog laugh, so that the water will come out of his mouth.'

'That's a splendid idea,' they all agreed. 'That is what we shall do.'

So they held auditions. The animals were very funny – first came the kookaburra. Now the kookaburra is a bird who makes a very strange sound, a loud cackling laugh which is really enough to make you laugh your head off when you hear him; he also tells very funny jokes. Well, he flew on to the platform in front of all the animals and he soon had them simply shrieking with laughter. If they hadn't been so short of water tears would have rolled down their faces.

'Oh yes, you'll do simply splendidly for the concert,' they shouted.

'Jolly good, well done!'

The duck-billed platypus played 'Waltzing Matilda' . . . tapping out the notes on the tortoise's back with his beak. And the Kangaroo did conjuring tricks, such as producing white rabbits from it's pouch.

Well, they all did their best to be amusing . . . surely the bull-frog would have to laugh . . .

'Now we must send an invitation to the frog and get him to come to the concert. We'll hold it tomorrow night as soon as the moon rises.'

The following night the stars were twinkling and the moon rose big and pale like a spotlight for their stage. The ground began to tremble and the huge bull-frog arrived in the forest clearing. He was so huge by now that he could hardly walk. His webbed feet were spread out flat, his great body shook and gurgled with the water and the warts on his back trembled like jellies.

He was quite unable to speak, of course, so he just sat and blinked at the animals in a lazy, full-up sort of way.

The concert began, the performers were exceedingly good. But, the bull-frog had absolutely no sense of humour. He just wouldn't laugh – he didn't think anything was funny. He just sat there, the ground shaking under him as the water inside him lapped and sloshed about while he sighed gently to himself.

The animals by now were so worried they couldn't laugh any more, they were really desperate. Suddenly there was a disturbance in the audience – the eel had arrived from goodness-knows-where. Of course, he'd come slithering and creeping under seats, in his usual slippery way.

'What's all this about?' he said.

He could hardly speak because he was so short of water his voice was very dry.

'Well,' said the animals, 'we're trying to make the bull-frog laugh to get the water out of him, but he doesn't like our jokes and he doesn't like our tricks and we're afraid that the whole event is a complete failure.'

'Oh,' said the eel. 'Don't worry about that, wait till he sees me dance.'

'Oh, you can't dance,' said the kangaroo. 'You haven't got any feet.'

'Now wait and see,' said the eel.

He slithered his way on to the platform leaving a little trail in the sand.

When he reached the stage, caught in the light of a bright moonbeam, he suddenly began to wiggle and wriggle and slither, and slide and bend, and curve and coil, and twist and dance, such a wonderful and fantastic fandango, tying himself in loops, in bows, in knots, you couldn't tell which was his head or which was his tail. He even stuck his tail half way down his throat and he bowled along like a hoop.

The bull-frog's eyes began to twinkle, the bull-frog began to shake, his great sides heaved, his great lips trembled. The animals watched him, their hearts thumping with anticipation. Would he laugh, or wouldn't he? There was a breathless pause. Suddenly the eel had a flash of inspiration. He bowled across the clearing and with the tip of his tail reached up and tickled the bull-frog under his chin. The eel had discovered the secret. Nothing in the world would make the bull-frog actually laugh except being tickled under the chin. He began to giggle and gurgle and splutter and – woosh – his mouth opened and he let out a great 'Ha, Ha' and an ocean of water came cascading from his lips.

Thc animals flung themselves under the rush of water. They splashed about, they washed themselves, they drank, they sported and floundered about in the torrents of the waterfall.

And from that time, the lakes and pools and streams in that part of Australia were never dry again. As for the bull-frog, no one ever saw him again. He left the theatre in disgust; perhaps he found another land and drank the water there, or perhaps he has begun to like sea water and lives in a cave at the bottom of the ocean.

A Small Adventure

'Mummy, Mummy, do you know what I've found?' said Jennifer, running into the kitchen.

'No darling, what?' said her mother looking up from her ironing at her daughter's excited face.

'An ant wearing a spotted coat.'

'Don't be daft,' yelled Nigel. He was her brother and three years older than she. 'It's not an ant with a spotted coat, it's a ladybird.'

'Oh,' said Jennifer in a small voice. Why was it he always knew the answers to everything? He seemed to be the cleverest person in the world and he was always making her feel stupid. She opened her fingers and looked at the small, spotted insect crawling in her palm.

It was very pretty with its shining spotted back and painted face. Jennifer peered at it through her glasses. She had to wear glasses because she had a squint, and the doctor said that if she wore them every day for a year or two her squint would go away and she would have pretty eyes when she became a young lady.

'Silly old four eyes!' jeered Nigel. 'She doesn't even know what a ladybird is.' And he went back to making his model aeroplane. Jennifer's hand closed gently round the insect again. She could feel her face going red and her eyes were starting to water.

'Nigel, stop teasing your sister,' said their mother. 'You didn't know what a ladybird was when you were Jenny's age, so stop boasting.'

Jennifer wandered out of the back door into the garden again. 'One day I'll be as clever as Nigel,' she muttered fiercely, 'and I'll be pretty too and I won't have to wear glasses, and then he won't laugh at me and call me four eyes.'

She felt the ladybird tickling her palm and very slowly opened her fingers and gazed through her spectacles at the dainty insect, blinking away her tears.

'Hello', said a tiny voice. 'Well, say hello, don't be rude. It's bad enough being shut in your dark hot hand, but I'll *really* take offence if you won't talk to me.'

Jennifer gave a little gasp. 'Is it you? Is it you, Ladybird, talking to me?'

'Of course it is, who did you think it was? There isn't anyone else around at the moment so it must be me.'

'Oh, how lovely,' Jennifer laughed. 'You can talk to me! Will you be my friend – my best friend?'

'I might be,' replied Ladybird in her high-pitched squeak, 'as long as you don't talk in such a huge booming voice, you're deafening me. Every time a human speaks I have to stuff my feelers in my ears.'

'Oh, I'm sorry,' said Jennifer, lowering her voice. 'I'll whisper from now on.'

'I say, that brother of yours is a bit rude, isn't he?' said Ladybird, giving her wings a little stretch: 'Oh don't worry, I'm not going to fly away, I just had a touch of wing cramp through being in your hand for so long.'

'Oh, Nigel's all right really,' said Jennifer, loyally. 'It's just that he knows a lot more things than I do because he's older than I am, but some day when I'm big and don't wear glasses, I'll be clever like him.'

'Well, I think you're pretty nice as you are, Jennifer,' squeaked Ladybird. 'And I love your glasses. I wish I had a pair with nice pink frames like that. If I were a bit bigger I'd ask to try them on, but I'm afraid they'd be too big for me.' Jennifer thought that was a great joke and nearly blew the ladybird out of her hand laughing.

'I'll tell you what,' said Ladybird. 'If you're very good and only speak in a whisper, I'll show you some secrets that Nigel doesn't know about.'

'Oh, will you really?' asked Jennifer, beginning to feel cheerful and excited. 'Will it be an adventure?'

'Well, yes, I suppose it will. A small adventure shall we say. You must do everything I say and you'll see. Now follow me.'

The ladybird fluttered from Jennifer's finger and floated off down the garden across the lawn to a flowerbed set beside the old red-brick wall. It was a very gay flowerbed filled with roses, marguerites, and dahlias of all colours, huge red pom poms, tiny pink buttons, bright yellow ones with faces as big as plates and some of the softest pink with petals that shot out like the rays of the sun. The dahlias were supported by sticks and on top of each stick, balancing somewhat drunkenly, was a plant pot. Ladybird alighted on the top of a plant pot and waited for Jennifer to catch up with her.

'Golly, I thought I'd lost you,' she whispered. 'Now what must I do?'

'You must tap three times on the plant pot, I want to introduce you to some friends.'

Jennifer gave three small knocks and before she had time to tie up a loose hair ribbon, a tiny brown face appeared through the hole at the top and asked, 'Who's that?'

'It's me, Jennifer. What's your name and who are you?'

'I'm 'Enry Earwig,' he said, crawling right out and displaying himself proudly on the top of the plant pot. 'How d'you like my weapons?' he asked, curling up his tail and proudly showing fearsome looking pincers.

'Very nice indeed,' said Jennifer, looking at them in awe.

'I'd swop 'em any day for your specs, I've always wanted a pair of specs. Still, they'd be a bit big for me.' Just then he caught sight of Ladybird who was watching all this with a smile.

''Ello there, old girl,' called 'Enry, ''ow's the world treating you? I'd invite you in but me and me friends have got something on – we're 'olding a "sit-in". I don't know quite what it means but we've been sitting in this old plant pot for about a month now and nothing's 'appened yet. Well, I'd better get back,' he said cheerfully, turning tail and giving his

pincers a flick. 'The others'll wonder where I've gone. Ta-ra-, nice to have met you, I'm sure.' And he disappeared into the hole again.

'Goodbye, Henry, I mean 'Enry,' said Jennifer, waving. Ladybird flew on to her shoulder and looked pleased. Jennifer had made a good impression. She would introduce her to someone else.

'Come on, Jennifer, there are more friends for you to meet. Go to the garden gate and then walk up the path towards the house. When you've got to the third paving stone you'll find a brick lying by the side of it. Pick it up and you shall see what you shall see.'

Jennifer carried out the instructions. She counted the paving stones carefully and then kneeling down she very gently lifted the brick. There was a terrific scurry underneath, creatures began hurrying in every direction. 'Oh, dear,' said Jennifer in dismay. 'I'm so sorry, I didn't mean to disturb you.'

'Oh, that's quite all right,' said one of the creatures. He was fat and grey with a scaley body and lots of little legs. 'It's just that we're not too keen on the light. It's inclined to hurt our eyes. If you bend over us and give us a bit of shade it might help.'

'But of course,' she said obligingly, leaning over them to shut out the sun.

'I'm Larry Woodlouse and these are my friends. Say how do you do everyone.' There was a chorus of 'Good afternoons' and 'Hellos' and a great deal of wiggling and scurrying, then one little woodlouse, who must have been a baby, asked 'What are those things on your nose?'

'They're my glasses for making my eyes go straight', replied Jennifer defensively.

'How smashing. I wish I had some to put on my nose,' said the baby woodlouse, and he began to dance round and round. Suddenly he became dizzy and fell on his back with his legs waving about in the air.

'Good gracious,' said his anxious mother, 'he's not on his back again is he? Really, it's too bad, I keep telling him not to get himself over-excited. The trouble is, once he's on his back he can't get up again,' and she gave him a shove.

'Don't worry,' whispered Jennifer, 'I'll help him.' And she looked around for a stick and levered the small creature back on to his feet again.

'Thank you very much, Miss,' said the mother. 'Now don't do that again, you naughty child. Next time there may not be anyone here to turn you the right way up again.'

Just then, Ambrose Ant put in an appearance.

'Hello, what's going on here?' he said all bright and beady.

Jennifer smiled at him and introduced herself. 'Ladybird here is introducing me to a few friends. It's quite exciting, I'd no idea she had so many.'

'Ahh, well you haven't met my gang yet have you?' he said, beckoning her on with a feeler. 'Just follow me and you shall see what you shall see.' He set off at quite a pace, scrambling over pebbles and boulders which must have seemed like huge mountains to him. Jennifer said 'goodbye' to the woodlice and replaced their brick.

'Come on, slow coach,' shouted Ambrose Ant.

'Don't dawdle, we ants always do everything as quickly as possible, it's the only way to get things done.'

Jennifer crawled after him on her hands and knees so as not to lose sight of him. He introduced her to William Worm and Sylvia Snail on the way and they seemed very charming and were full of admiration for her spectacles. Jennifer felt quite proud of having to wear them now. After all it's not everyone who gets the chance to wear something unusual like spectacles, is it? Ambrose led her to the corner of the lawn and told her to watch carefully. Soon she saw a long thin line of ants approaching like a row of smartly turned out soldiers, one behind the other in neat array.

'This is the gang,' said Ambrose, waving a feeler proudly. 'Quite a smart lot, don't you think? I give the orders round here you know. Company, halt!' he boomed. The ants came to a standstill and saluted Jennifer. 'At ease,' screamed Ambrose. The tension dropped a little and the ants waved a feeler or two.

'Um, er, permission to speak, sir,' said one particularly bold ant. 'Um, what are those things on that lady's face?'

'Those, you ignorant fool, are glasses,' Ambrose snapped back; turning to Jennifer he said, 'You have to be firm with them you know or they get out of hand. There are so many of them you see, we don't want mutiny.'

'I quite understand,' said Jennifer.

'Well, sir,' said the inquisitive ant, 'I'd just like to say that I think they look particularly smart. Why can't we all be issued with them?'

'Because you can't,' barked Ambrose. 'Attention, you lazy lot. Now I want you to carry this bread crumb the birds have left back to the nest immediately.'

Jennifer watched in amazement as the ants formed a little circle and began to carry the bread crumb away with a great deal of heave-ho-ing. It was the size of a huge boulder to them but it seemed that no task was too great for these tiny insects. Ambrose followed them, shouting orders and rounding up the few lazy ones who were pretending to help but weren't really helping at all. Jennifer waved, she was quite sad to see them go. Just then Ladybird flew back on to her shoulder in a great state of distress.

'Come quickly,' she squealed. 'One of my friends is in trouble, he's fallen into the water.'

'Oh, no,' said Jennifer, and ran quickly to the lily pool, her plaits flying behind her. Ladybird pointed to a small black beetle swimming bravely though not very well.

'If you don't get him out quickly,' wailed Ladybird, 'the goldfish will eat him or he'll drown.'

Jennifer felt panicky – what should she do? She looked around for a stick but there wasn't one near so she ran to the garden shed shouting 'Tell him to hang on if he can, I shan't be a second.'

'Hang on, Bertie,' called Ladybird from an overhanging weed, 'we'll save you.'

Bertie Beetle was floundering a little now, a ring of tiny bubbles was forming round him and a mysterious golden shadow was gliding about under the water. The fish!

Ladybird was beside herself. 'Be quick, Jennifer, he's going.' Jennifer pounded back across the lawn with her fishing net. Poor Bertie had just gone down for the second time and the golden shadow, like a small painted shark, was slipping nearer and nearer.

The other insects were crowding round the edge of the pool, shouting encouragements and waving their legs and feelers in horror. Jennifer dipped in her net and brushed the fish aside just as his jaws were about to snack at Bertie's flailing legs. Then she carefully caught the little beetle in the mesh, lifted him out of the water and shook him out gently on to the lawn.

All the insects held their breath; had he died? Was the shock too much for him? Bertie gave a shudder and stretched his waterlogged legs, then looking at Jennifer with a weak little smile he gurgled in a watery voice, 'Those are the nicest spectacles I've ever seen.'

The insects squeaked, cheered, spread wings, rubbed their legs together, rattled their mandibles, buzzed, whirred, and all agreed that Jennifer was the heroine of the day. She'd never felt so happy. Just then, her mother called her in for tea. She waved goodbye to the insects and blew a kiss to Ladybird after settling her on a hollyhock leaf.

'Goodbye, Ladybird. I'll see you again soon, I hope,' she called and ran inside. Nigel was still making his model.

'Hello, four eyes,' he said, without looking up. 'How's your spotty ant?'

Jennifer didn't care, she smiled a secret smile. She

was perfectly happy and now she knew about lots of things that Nigel didn't know about and never would, and what's more, she was proud of her spectacles. She had had a lovely small adventure.

Granny Green's Mud Frock

One Monday morning Sophie's mother said, 'Today I am going to take you over to spend the day with Granny because it's Monday and I've such a lot of things to do. I have a large wash and in the afternoon I have to go shopping to buy a birthday present for Daddy.' Sophie was very happy because she loved to visit her Granny. She helped her Mummy to get ready, struggling to fasten the toggles on her duffle-coat and sticking her feet into her Wellingtons. You see Granny Green lived in the country.

'Make sure she comes warmly wrapped with something sensible on her feet,' Granny Green had said on the telephone. 'It's ankle-deep in mud out here, because of all the rain we've been having.'

'Oh good,' laughed Sophie when her mother told her. 'I love mud.'

'I know you do, but please don't get yourself too dirty and don't make a muddy mess in Granny's house.'

They caught the bus at the end of the street and it

took them away from the houses into the country where Granny Green's cottage sat, right in the middle of a field. When Sophie jumped down from the bus she looked at the ground, and then up at her mother and said in a disappointed voice, 'I'm not ankle-deep in mud, where is it?'

'You wait 'til we walk up the path to Granny's house, you'll soon see the mud.'

She took Sophie's hand and sure enough once through the gate it was very muddy indeed. It was all soft and squelchy, Sophie's boots made lovely sucking noises as she splattered along. There were big puddles too, dark and glassy reflecting the sun and the clouds. Sophie bent down to peer into a pool and saw her own face staring back.

'Hallo, me,' she said.

'Sophie, do hurry dear,' her mother called, 'It's getting late and I must get back to do the washing. Don't walk in the middle where the mud is thick. Keep to the edges.'

Sophie didn't want to keep to the edges, it was such a good feeling to go plodding through the stickiness, looking back at the patterns made by the soles of her Wellingtons. Granny Green, whose cottage was white with a green front door, was standing on the step waiting for them. She kissed Sophie's mother and then she kissed Sophie, and Sophie thought how nice Granny smelt, of violets and face powder.

'Take off your Wellies, darling,' she said 'and leave them on the step. My word, they are dirty aren't they.'

'Yes,' said Sophie and added triumphantly, 'I've got splashes up the back of my legs too.'

Inside her warm kitchen Granny found an old towel and wiped the splatters off Sophie's legs, then she made Mummy a cup of coffee while Sophie stroked Tootums the kitten, who was sleeping in front of the fire.

When Sophie's mother had gone back home Granny Green said, 'Now, I'm going to make you something to eat, Sophie. Would you like sausages and mashed potatoes?'

Well, that was just what Sophie liked to eat best of all. She was happy because she knew that Granny Green would give her fruit and jelly afterwards and that was delicious too. She ate up her dinner carefully and Tootums the kitten sat by the fire watching her with his big yellow eyes, hoping she'd drop a piece of sausage on the carpet, but she didn't. She didn't spill tomato sauce on the tablecloth either.

Granny Green cleared the table and said to Sophie, 'What would you like to do now, shall we get out the jigsaw puzzle?'

'No, I don't think so,' said Sophie.

'Would you like to play shops?'

'No, I don't think so,' said Sophie.

'Shall we make a necklace from the bead-box?'

'No, I don't think so,' said Sophie.

'Well, you tell me, what would you like to do?'

'I'd like to play in the mud,' said Sophie.

'Play in the mud, I see,' said Granny Green, not in the least bit surprised.

'Well now, what would Mummy say if you got your clothes all dirty?'

'I don't know,' said Sophie, 'I think she would be cross.'

'I'm sure she would,' said Granny Green, 'now, let me think.'

She rocked backwards and forwards in the rocking-chair for a while, suddenly she jumped up and said, 'I know, come with me.'

She led Sophie up the tiny staircase into her room, where she rummaged through a deep drawer full of woollies.

'Here we are,' she said, 'just the thing.'

She held up an old stripey jumper, it was very old and a bit holey but she pulled it over Sophie's head, and then stood back and looked at her grand-daughter, smiling. It was Granny Green's old jumper and it was too big, but it completely covered up Sophie's clothes and it was long enough to reach to her ankles. Granny Green rolled up the sleeves so that Sophie's hands stuck through. Then she found an old piece of ribbon, and tying it round the middle, hitched up the jumper so that it wouldn't trail on the ground.

'Now then, that's what I call an excellent mud-frock,' she said.

As Sophie pulled on her Wellingtons she felt very happy. Granny Green always seemed to know what girls and boys liked to do, but that was probably because she was very old and very clever. The mud was beautiful, there was a large juicy patch of it quite near the front door. Sophie stuck in a tentative boot and felt it sink in with a satisfying squelch. Then she took a step forward until both her feet sank – yes – up to the ankles. She took a few more steps. Then she gave a squeak because one of her boots was stuck, she pulled hard and, plop! Her foot shot out of the Wellington, but the Wellington stayed behind, glued fast in the mud. Granny Green looked out of the window and laughed at Sophie who was standing on one foot like a duck at the water's edge. She opened the window and shouted, 'Stay there Sophie, I'll come and help you.'

When the boot had been retrieved and replaced, Sophie thought she'd see how it felt to touch the mud with her hands, she bent down and stuck her finger into it. It was smooth and damp and thick, she pulled the finger out. It was all black. Then feeling rather daring, she plunged her hand into the mud and holding up a black fistful waved it at Granny, who called, 'Why don't you make some mud pies?'

Sophie looked pleased. 'Yes,' she said 'that would be nice.'

She squeezed the mud and watched with delight as it oozed between the cracks in her fingers. Then she rolled it in her hands till it made a ball and threw it – slap – back into the mud pool. Droplets of water splashed back over her mud-frock and on to her nose. Sophie giggled, and tried to wipe them off with the back of her hand, leaving a big black smear right across her cheek. Granny Green laughed a lot and came out of the kitchen door with some patty tins.

'Here you are, make me some mud pies in these.'

Sophie poured puddle-water into the mud from an old jam jar she had found. She stirred it all up with a piece of stick until it was good and thick, then she worked very hard, squeezing and pressing the mud into the tins. Then she decorated each pie with a

small stone. It took her a long time because the mud was so lovely to hold, so mushy and squashy, so cool and clammy, so good to mould into shapes. She rolled it in her palms and she made a long mud sausage, and she made a few mud apples as well.

'Look Granny, I've finished the pies and I've made a sausage and some apples too.'

'They're very good,' exclaimed Granny Green. 'Leave them in the sun to bake.'

When it was time for tea Granny filled the kitchen sink with warm water, pulled off the mud-frock and dumped Sophie on the draining board. She washed the mud from Sophie's hands and face and then she washed the sock which had got all muddy when the Wellington came off and put it into the airing cupboard to dry. When Mummy came back to collect her Sophie was as clean as a little girl could be. Mummy was puzzled when Sophie showed the things she had made.

'How did you manage to make such lovely mud pies and still keep clean?' she asked.

'Ah,' said Granny Green eyeing the mud-frock rolled in a ball by the sink, 'that's our secret, isn't it Sophie?'

Sophie just giggled.

Horrible Harold and the Bubblegum

Harold stared through the glass top of the sweet-shop counter at the assortment of delicious goodies. There was a box of sherbert fountains, long ribbons and pipes of liquorice, sticks of candy, coloured gob-stoppers, twopenny chews, chocolate cigarettes, dolly mixtures, and dozens of other sweets that he liked; but the thing Harold loved best he was forbidden to have – and that was bubblegum. His mother's advice still echoed in his mind.

'Here's ten pence Harold. Go down to the sweet shop and buy something for yourself but don't you dare get any of that filthy bubblegum; or chewing gum either, if it comes to that.'

The ten pence was clutched tightly in his damp palm as his eyes darted over the delicious display.

'Well, Harold, have you decided?' asked Mrs Bell, the shopkeeper, in a patient voice. He's been staring for about ten minutes, and she'd served at least five other people whilst he'd been choosing.

'Ummmm . . . Yes,' he answered slowly. 'I'll have a lollipop, ummmm, two liquorice chews, a roll of aniseed balls, and eh . . .' 'Yes, Harold,' said Mrs Bell, hiding her impatience, 'And err, two bubblegums,' he blurted out in a large voice, his face going rather red.

She slid open the glass panel, collected the chosen sweets and put them in a small paper-bag. Harold handed over the ten pence and ran out of the shop, feeling a mixture of guilt and pleasure. He ran all the way home, up the stairs and into his bedroom, closing the door behind him quietly. Then he sat on his bed, emptied the paper-bag and laid his purchases in neat order, admiring his choice and gloating over each in turn. He undid the cellophane at the top of the aniseed balls and tried one. It was delicious. He rolled it round his tongue and sucked it slowly until there was only a pearl left which he crunched between well-filled molars. Then he had one of the chews, deliciouly orange-flavoured, and a couple of licks at his lollipop, strawberry; but his whole heart's desire was centred on – yes – the bubblegum. He peeped out of the door to make sure no one was coming; he knew his mother was downstairs talking to their neighbour, Auntie Kath, so he carefully took off the paper which he hid under the mattress and popped the lump of pink gum into his mouth. It was gorgeous.

He chewed away until it was a nice soft gooey consistency, then he sat down in front of the dressing-table, pressed the tip of his tongue into the centre of the sticky ball and blew – a small, pink bubble emerged, round and rubbery, and he quickly sucked it back in. He had a few more practice blows, but he wasn't satisfied because he knew he was the champion bubble-blower in the street, and he was longing to blow a gigantic one; so drawing a deep breath he arranged the gum in an expert manner on the end of his tongue and blew out. A lovely, big, fat bubble emerged, the size of a small balloon. He went on blowing softly but he'd misjudged it and . . . splat . . . it burst and the thin sticky skin splattered all over his face.

'Cripes!' he muttered, pulling out a grubby handkerchief and scrubbing hard at his face. It was dreadful trying to get it off; he scraped at it with his nails and peeled it off in little strips. It was all over his fingers now, and, horror of horrors, he could hear his mother coming up the stairs . . .

'Harold, where are you? I want you to run to the shops and get me a drum of salt and some cornflakes,' she called.

He pulled the rest of the gum out of his mouth; it was very soft and warm and he couldn't get it off his fingers, it was joining all of them together in long pink strings. The more he pulled and clawed at it the more entangled he became. He crawled under the bed and lay there holding his breath. His mother opened the door, gave a little 'tutt' of impatience and went away again. Harold lay on his back rubbing his hands together until most of the gum had reassembled into a ball again, then he stuck it on a bed spring and began to crawl out backwards; but he felt something tugging at him, the horrid stuff has stuck to his hair. He gazed in alarm at the stiff angry tuft of hair standing upright from the centre of his head and realized that this was the point of no return. He knew from experience that it was quite impossible to get bubblegum out of his hair. He crept into the bathroom, found his mother's nail scissors and snipped away at the tangled mess throwing it down the lavatory and pulling the chain. He looked horrible – there was a dreadful stubby place right in the middle of his head which his mother would notice without a doubt.

By now Harold was throwing caution to the wind, and he put his head under the cold tap and then pulled the long bits of hair over his bald patch, smarming them down with soap. Actually, it didn't look too bad and after he'd given his face a scrub he looked fairly respectable. Feeling rather pleased with himself, he grabbed his other bubblegum and ran downstairs.

'I'm here, Mum,' he shouted cheerfully, 'I've just been having a wash. I'll go and do that shopping for you now.'

His mother's eyes opened wide in amazement. She'd never known Harold to wash himself before without having to be forced, and she wondered if he was feeling quite well. She gave him some money and a shopping bag and he set off down the garden path whistling loudly. When he was through the garden gate and round the corner, he fished in his pocket for the second bubblegum, unwrapped it and put it in his mouth. He was very happy. His mother hadn't noticed the awful hole in his hair or the traces of gum on his face and hands. It was a bright windy day, puffs of cloud were blowing gaily across a bright blue sky and leaves were swirling round his feet. The gum in his mouth was becoming a good consistency and was still full of flavour. He had a few small practice blows trying to whistle at the same time without much success and then said aloud to himself: 'I'm going to blow the biggest bubble that's ever been blown.'

Someone passing looked at him strangely and he realized he must seem a little odd talking to himself. Then he prepared the gum in his mouth and began to blow. At first it was just a tiny baby bubble like the ones that sometimes fly out of detergent bottles, and then it grew into the size of a medium tomato. Harold's cheeks puffed out, now it was as large as a honeydew melon. A little more air and it was the size of a football; he felt very pleased with himself.

'Cripes,' he thought, 'This really is going to be the biggest bubblegum bubble that's ever been blown.'

He allowed the pink ball attached to his lips to grow even bigger. He was bursting with pride. 'Cor, I wish my pals could see me now,' he thought, 'I must hold the world record for bubblegum blowing.'

Suddenly, Harold felt a strange sensation as though he were being sucked upwards by some magical force. He was whisked off his feet and began a smooth and swift ascent past the garden fences above the doors and windows of his neighbours' houses, past the bus stops and the chimney pots and the red tiles and up above the trees and lamp-posts, suspended by the balloon billowing dangerously from his lips. He peered down at the chimneys below, he didn't dare to call, for he knew that if the gum burst he would crash down on to the pavement, now a thin ribbon of grey below him.

Harold's heart was pounding. He had just floated past the church tower – he'd never had such a good view of the weathercock. Actually it looked a bit rusty when you got close to it. His lips were aching through being in a goldfish position and the wind whistling round him was terribly cold. He felt frightened. He wished he'd listened to his mother. He knew he was in a most dangerous predicament. A large crow flew past him and was so surprised it flew back and circled him a couple of times, glaring and cawing in amazement.

'Oh, it's all right for you,' thought Harold, 'You know how to land, but what's going to happen to me, I'll land with a terrible crunch and that will be that.' He suddenly felt quite terrified and his heart nearly jumped out of his mouth when he looked down and saw that he was floating over Simon's garden. Simon was his dreaded enemy. He was standing on the circular lawn in his garden gazing upwards at Harold, a horrible grin on his face, armed with his bow and arrow.

'Help!' thought Harold, unable to shout because of the bubble in his mouth. 'Surely he won't shoot.' But Simon was hooting with glee and began to take aim; he drew back the string and with a whoop of delight let the arrow fly towards poor Harold's balloon. His aim was true, there was a loud plop, the gum spread evenly over Harold's face, covering his cheeks and eyes and hair and he felt himself falling and falling as if in a ghastly dream. He landed fairly softly as it happened in the springy arms of a fir tree in Simon's garden. He felt himself caught in the friendly branches, swayed for a bit and then crashed gently through on to the soft earth beneath.

Simon was contrite. It occurred to him that he

might have done Harold a serious injury. He brushed the pine needles from Harold's back, apologized and shook hands. He began to think Harold was rather a brave boy because he didn't cry or complain. Actually he was too winded to speak.

When Harold walked into the kitchen his mother looked up from her washing and scowled – he was a dreadful sight, his whole face was covered in a mask of bubblegum.

'You've been at it again, I see,' yelled his mother. 'You naughty boy, I told you never to buy that disgusting conglomeration again. Now get up to bed at once and stay there for the rest of the day.'

Harold was quite glad to lie down on his soft, comfortable bed. He tried to peel a little of the gum off but he was so tired he fell asleep. Needless to say, he didn't buy bubblegum again, or chewing gum either if it comes to that.

The Old Lady and the Tramp

An Old Story from Sweden

This is a story told to the children of Sweden.

One day an old tramp was walking along in the middle of winter through a dark forest and it was beginning to get rather late; the sun had set, it was already twilight, and it was bitterly cold. But he was a jolly tramp – he whistled a merry tune and he felt cheerful because he could see, twinkling away in the distance, a little light.

'There's a house over there,' he said to himself. 'Surely whoever lives in it will let me sleep the night by their fire and give me something to eat.'

The light came from the window of a cottage and soon the tramp was knocking on the door. It was opened by a fat, rather cross-looking woman.

'What do you want then?'

'Please, madam, I've walked a long way. I'm very cold, I'm very tired and the next house must be a good five miles away. Please let me come in and sleep on the floor until it gets light, because it's very cold out here in the forest.'

'What do you think this is then, an inn or

something? I live here all by myself, I'm not going to let in a stranger.'

'I promise you, madam, I'm a very respectable man. I won't do you harm. I won't steal anything.'

'I should think not indeed,' said the old lady. 'You won't get a chance because you won't even get through the door.'

'Oh, don't be hard-hearted, lady,' said the tramp. 'Remember we should help one another.'

'Help one another! And where would I be if I helped every tramp that came to my door? I'd be eaten out of house and home. Go on, be off with you.'

But the tramp was very persistent, and he argued and argued with her until finally she was so tired and the open door was letting such a draught into the house that she said 'Oh, all right then, come in. You can sleep on the floor. I certainly haven't got a bed for you.'

'Oh, I knew you were a good, kind woman the minute I set eyes on you,' he said.

When he got in the house he saw that the old lady, although she pretended not to have much food or much money, was actually just being rather mean. She had a very cosy cottage and a nice big log fire glowing on the hearth.

The tramp sat himself down in front of it, the steam rose from his damp clothes. He warmed his gnarled hands in front of the flames and blew on his fingers to get the feeling back into them.

'Oh, dear, it's a very cold night out there. You don't know how happy I am to be all cosy and warm inside.'

'All right, don't go on about it,' she said. 'Just sit there and keep quiet.'

The old tramp was beginning to feel rather hungry. 'I hope you don't mind if I ask, madam, but ummmm . . . have you err . . . got just a little crust or two that I could eat?'

'I've told you that you could come in here and sleep on the floor, I didn't say you were going to eat. I've hardly anything in the cupboard for myself, so it's not likely that I'd be giving what I've got to a tramp is it?'

'I could cook myself something, if it would save you any trouble.'

'Cook yourself something! Certainly not. I'm not having you messing up my kitchen.'

'But it wouldn't take me very long, and I wouldn't made a mess I promise you. All I need is a nice big pan and some water.'

'Oh, a nice big pan and some water. Oh well, if you're so clever you can make a meal out of a pan of water, I'll get one for you.' And the old lady went to her cupboard, pulled out her biggest pan, filled it with cold water and gave it to the tramp.

The tramp put the pan on the fire.

'Oh, thank you lady. Now I'm going to show you how to make some lovely soup. Now let me see.'

He put his hand in his pocket and pulled out an assortment of things – a conker, a piece of string, a pocket knife, a handkerchief, a couple of brown feathers and a four-inch nail. He sorted amongst them, picked out the four-inch nail and dropped it into the pan of water.

'And what do you think you're doing now?' said

the old lady.

'Well, madam, I'm making myself some nail soup.'

'Nail soup? Whoever heard of such a thing?'

'But madam I can assure you it's the most delicious soup you've ever tasted.' And he unhooked a big wooden spoon from the wall and began to stir the water and the nail round and round. Then he took a sip from the spoon.

'Mmmmm, not bad, not bad really for nail soup. It'd taste a bit better if it had a bit of barley in it, but as nail soup goes it's not bad.'

'Huh, well, as a matter of fact I have got a little bit of barley somewhere.'

'Have you, madam? Could you spare me just a handful to throw in to thicken it up a bit, you know.'

'Oh, all right,' said the old lady, rather intrigued. And she bustled away and came back with a jar filled with barley and shook a few grains into the pot.

'Oh, thank you madam. You really are very kind,' said the tramp. He stirred and tasted again. 'Mmmm yes, that's coming along well. Mind you it'd taste better if we added a little flour just, well, to give a bit more richness like; you know, nail soup really needs a bit of flour.'

'Well, I might, I might have just a spoonful of flour somewhere,' said the old lady; and she came back with a little bag of flour and shook it into the pan.

'Oh thank you madam,' he said, stirring it and watching it get thicker. Now this is really something. I'll let you have a taste of this nail soup.'

'Ooh fancy,' she said. 'Look at it, it looks quite

nice. Look at what you can make of just a nail eh?'

'Well, it's amazing madam, it really is, what you can make out of a nail. It, umm, it would be a bit better mind you if I could just have a little bit of salt-beef and a couple of vegetables you know? A potato, a carrot or something like that, just to add a bit of flavour to it. You see, I've used this nail to make soup about six times this week and I think there's not really much flavour coming out of it, not as much as one would like anyway.'

'Oh well, just stay there. I'll see what I've got,' said the fat old lady, bustling away. She came back with a chopped up onion, six carrots, five potatoes and two lumps of salted meat.

'Just put these in and see how they go, see if that's enough.' She threw them into the pan.

'Oh, thank you, thank you, madam, that should be quite nice. Yes, yes.'

The tramp stirred and tasted. 'Mmmm, that's much better, it's bringing out the flavour of the nail, you see it's giving it more of a soupee, nailee, brothee sort of taste if you get my meaning.'

'May I have a taste then?' she asked.

'Well, madam, I would like you to have a bowlful of this but really this soup has got to be fit for, well, gentlefolk before I let you taste it and it really needs a drop of milk in it before it's up to standard.'

'Oh, I see, it's funny you should say that. You see, my cow just calved the other day so I do happen to have a little drop of milk, but I'll have to slip outside for it.'

The old lady took up her lantern and opened the door. The wind blew everything off the table but she

soon hurried back with a jug of milk and poured it into the pan.

'I think this is the real finishing touch, madam. Yes, yes, it's just perfect,' and the tramp licked his lips.

'Well, I never did. Fancy soup out of a nail,' she exclaimed.

'Now then, madam, bring a bowl over.'

'Oh, thank you. You've really taught me something tonight,' said the old lady, bringing across a couple of blue striped bowls and setting them down on the hearth.

The tramp ladled out the soup and they both sat down together in front of the warm glow. As they supped the delicious broth the old lady said, 'I mean, it's so cheap and economical isn't it? Just some water and a nail, and well a few bits and pieces I suppose. But mostly it's the nail.'

She felt so pleased that she thought she'd better put something towards it, so she hurried away and came back with slices of meat and cheese and butter and bread, and soon the table was laden like a feast. It was just like Christmas – they drank a bottle of wine from her best glasses. Soon they'd eaten their fill and drank until they were merry and warm and happy.

The tramp, quite content, lay down on the floor to go fast asleep in front of the fire, but the old lady said to him 'Oh no, after you made such lovely nail soup, and we've had such an enjoyable evening, I think I might as well offer you a good bed.'

She took him to the little spare room under the eaves and he snuggled down into a warm and cosy bed.

'Goodnight, madam. Thank you very much,' he said. And he clasped in his hand the four-inch nail he had fished out of the pan before she emptied the last dregs away.

'Oh, that's all right – I mean, after all we must help one another, mustn't we?' she said, as she closed the door softly behind her.

Michael and His Friends

Michael lay in his hot bed quite still, counting the patterns on his wallpaper. There were a hundred and fifty-six roses each with five leaves across the wall, and alternately one hundred and fifty-five daisies each with a stalk and three leaves.

He had counted them five times that morning and twice they had come out the same, so that must be right. He was in bed with the flu and he felt awful, his throat was sore, his head was hot and heavy and he had a most annoying cough. His nose kept running too, and it was quite red and sore on the end through blowing it.

Michael sighed and looked out of the window; it was winter and the trees, quite bare of leaves, were motionless in the damp, chill air. Michael turned away and looked at the wall again. It was warm in his room and he felt rather sweaty. He tried reading his bumper annual for a while but he practically knew it all off by heart so that was a bit boring. Then he did some crayoning, but he had to sit up to do that which made him feel worse and worse so he pushed his crayoning book away, slid down in the bed and waited. He could hear his mother downstairs and he tried to work out what she was doing. The radio was playing pop music and he could hear that she was singing and rattling pans and crockery.

'I expect she's making the lunch,' he thought. 'Oh dear, I don't feel very hungry. I'll count the pattern on the wall again and see if she comes up before I've finished.'

He had reached seventy-five roses when a tray appeared round the door followed by his mother, her face all smiles and twinkly eyes. 'How's my boy?' she said, crossing towards the bed. 'Come along, sit up. I've made you some nice soup and a glass of blackcurrant juice.'

Michael inwardly groaned – he knew he couldn't eat a bite. 'And you can have some custard and stewed apple afterwards if you feel like it,' said his mother, settling the tray on his lap and plumping up the pillows behind him. Then she whisked out of the door and sang all the way downstairs.

Michael looked at his tray in dismay. She had made it look so nice for him; there was a checked tray-cloth and a paper napkin folded like a lily, and a bowl of soup with carrots and peas and little spaghetti stars swimming around in it. There was a tall glass clinking with ice cubes full of dark-red blackcurrant juice, and a plate of toast fingers. Normally he would have gulped it all down in a few seconds and wanted more, but today he had no appetite at all. He hated to disappoint her, and tried the soup. But after one spoonful he felt quite sick.

He sipped the blackcurrant juice – that was better. He managed to swallow half a glass of that and the coldness of it soothed his throat, but the toast he just couldn't manage at all. He sat and thought for a moment and then he carefully worked his way out of the blankets, and wriggled on to the floor without spilling anything. He had an idea: 'I'll empty it out of the window, then she won't know I haven't eaten it.'

Standing up was awful, he felt very dizzy. He wrapped his dressing-gown tightly round him, crept over to the window and looked out. He could see his own garden and two others, one on each side. They were very bare and still. Some shirts and tea towels hung on the neighbour's washing line, stiff as cardboard with the cold. The lily pond had a thin skin of ice. Michael quickly slipped the latch and pushed the window open. He fetched his soup bowl and emptied it out into the holly bush below – he saw the squares of carrot and turnip decorate the glossy leaves and then slip off on to the soil in a cloud of steam. Then the toast fingers joined them. He closed the window very quickly, took off his dressing-gown and jumped back into his warm bed. He listened for his mother but she was still singing away rattling china and pans.

After a while Michael fell asleep. He didn't know what woke him, he only knew that his eyes were open and he felt a lot better. He glanced around, the tray had gone and a strange bright light was coming in from the window. Large white flakes were floating past, swiftly, softly. It was snowing. Michael was happy and excited. The branches of the chestnut tree were bare no longer, they were decked in a rim of

crisp white snow. The flakes were swirling with such depth and thickness, daisies in a summer field, blossom petals in the wind, stars in the universe. Michael gasped with delight and ran to the window, a fine powder covered the gardens, even the lily pond was white. He hoped he would be better before it melted and disappeared. He loved playing in the snow. Then something else caught his attention, a little sparrow had fluttered on to the window sill and started pecking. His tiny beak went tap-tap-tap on the ledge. Michael wondered what he'd found to eat and then he realized it was some crumbs from his toast fingers that had been scattered there by mistake. He watched the little bird with delight, as it puffed out its feathers and looked at him with black beady eyes. When the crumbs had gone it flew away with a whirr of wings and vanished into the snow flakes.

Michael returned to his crayoning and felt much better and quite cheerful. His mother came into the room and looked at him with a gentle smile.

'Do you know,' she said, 'A little bird just told me that you threw your soup and toast fingers out of the window into the holly tree. You can't have felt very hungry. Perhaps you feel like having some tea now.'

Michael was sure it couldn't have been his little friend who had given him away. Actually, his mother had been at the kitchen window when he had emptied his food out and she'd seen it fly past and land in the holly bush. But she couldn't be cross with him, not when he felt ill.

It snowed all night, the gardens looked beautiful next morning, sparkling with frost and icicles in the bright winter sun.

Michael gazed at it with longing. It was so boring being ill in bed. He wished he was better and could go out and play. Then, quite suddenly he heard 'tap-tap', on the window pane. His eyes widened in surprise. There, as brave as can be was the little sparrow, his feathers fluffed out against the cold, his beady eyes searching for crumbs on the window ledge. Michael was so pleased to see him again. He crushed one of his biscuits into crumbs, and wrapping the eiderdown around him opened the window and scattered them about on the ledge. The bird flew away of course, but as soon as the window was closed it returned and began to peck away busily. Soon the sparrow was joined by a pair of blue tits and a rather bossy robin, and finally with a great deal of flap and fuss by a big fat pigeon. Quite a bit of chirping and arguing went on as to who was going to eat the most, but it was all very entertaining. It cheered Michael up watching them and seeing how the tiny birds tried to out-do the big fat pigeon.

He fed them every day. They grew to expect the titbits and every morning they fluttered around the window waiting for their breakfasts. By now all the birds in the garden seemed to know about the delicious meals. There was a blackbird now, and a thrush, and several rowdy starlings. Michael came to know them all and watched them peck and preen on the frozen ledge.

Soon he was quite well again, the doctor said he could go out and play as long as he wore an overcoat and muffler. It was marvellous to be running about outside again. He built a snowman, threw snowballs, and made a slide down the path. But he never forgot his little friends who had cheered him up and helped him to get better.

All through the winter when the ground was hard and the pond frozen, Michael spread crumbs for them until the spring came and they flew away to build their nests.

Ewungelema

An Old African Story

Here is a story that is told to the children of Zambia in Africa.

Once upon a time there was a famine in Africa, there was no food to be had at all and all the animals were starving.

Now in the centre of a great forest was a magic tree, and the animals knew that this tree would feed them with wonderful fruit if only they could remember its name, but as there hadn't been a famine for many hundreds of years, no one had had to call the name of the magic tree for a very long time, and so it was forgotten and not one of the animals could remember it.

One evening all the starving animals gathered together at the foot of the tree. They racked their brains and scratched their heads, and tried all sorts of made-up names in the hope that they might guess the right one, like Poonji-Poonji and Scoobie-Diddle, but the tree just remained with its arms spread wide and no fruit on it at all.

‘I’ve suddenly had a terribly good idea,’ said the lion. ‘Somewhere in the dim darkness of my memory I remember my great-great-grandfather saying that the mountain spirit knew the name of the tree. We must send one of the swifter animals in search of the mountain spirit to ask him what it is.’

It was decided to send the hare because he was such a fast runner. So, gathering his little furry body together, he set off at a tremendous pace and found the mountain spirit. He bowed low, feeling really rather frightened, and said in a humble voice ‘Oh, oh mountain spirit, all my animal friends are dying of hunger and we’ve forgotten the name of the magic tree – could you tell us what it is?’

‘Mmm, yes, well you see the name of the tree is Ewungelema. Ewungelema, little creature. Now have you understood that? Are you sure? Well, go back to the forest quickly before you forget it.’

‘Thanks,’ said the hare. And he turned quickly and with his white tail bobbing he fled back to his friends. He ran as fast as his legs could carry him, when all of a sudden . . . bang, crash, woosh . . . tipsy-turvy, head-over-heels, stars flashing, lights twinkling, the little hare had run headlong into a huge anthill and knocked himself quite silly. He made the rest of the journey reeling about and stumbling over his paws.

‘Well, well? What was the name, quickly . . .’ asked the animals.

‘Uh, oh, oh dear, I’ve forgotten.’

‘Stupid creature,’ they said. ‘Now what are we

going to do? Oh dear, we shall have to send someone else.'

'Who shall we send?'

'Let's send the buffalo. He's got a bigger head and perhaps a bigger brain. He'll remember the name.'

So the great hairy, huffing, puffing, lumbering buffalo turned round and slowly galloped off into the sunset. When he reached the mountain spirit he went down on his big hairy knees and said 'Oh mountain spirit, I'm afraid the hare forgot the name of the magic tree and so they've sent me along instead. Would you mind repeating the name of the tree again?'

'Uugghhh,' sighed the mountain spirit. 'How silly you animals are, the name of the magic tree is Ewungelema. Now have you got that? Don't forget it and hurry back to your friends before you do.'

So the buffalo, overjoyed, set off in his great lumbering stride, trundled down the mountain humming a little tune to himself as he went, watching the flies that were buzzing round his nose.

It's a pity he did because – crash, bang, stumble, down he went. He too had run straight into the ant-hill.

'Ooh, ooh, my goodness me,' he said, pulling himself together. 'What a shock, I feel quite dizzy. Oh, what was I supposed to be doing? That's right, I was supposed to be remembering the name of the magic tree and now it's gone straight out of my head.

Whatever shall I say to the other animals?'

Well, of course, the other animals were beside themselves with rage.

'We shall all be dead soon,' they said, 'unless we get the name of the tree.'

The old lion who had first spoken about the mountain spirit stepped forward and shook his huge and shaggy mane.

'There's nothing for it but I shall have to go myself. I'm getting a bit old for this sort of thing; I'm weak with hunger and very, very tired. However, as I seem to be the only sensible animal around here I shall return at dawn with the name of the magic tree. Goodbye friends.' And he set off loping through the twilight.

When he reached the mountain spirit he said, 'I'm afraid you'll have to forgive my friends. The buffalo has forgotten the name too, so I thought I'd better bring myself along. It's no good trusting these lesser beings. They haven't got my brains you know. Be a sport old man, tell me the name of the magic tree?'

'The name is Ewungelema,' cried the spirit. 'Go back to the forest quickly and don't forget it.'

'Oh thanks,' said the lion. 'You really are a GRRR-REAT spirit,' and he loped off down the mountain side. He felt very pleased with himself, exceedingly important, noble, royal. But pride comes before a fall, and crash, down he went helter-skelter, head-over-heels, big paws floundering in the air – and his head yes, buried in the ant-hill.

'Ugh, these horrid creatures are up my nose and in

my mouth. Atishoo! Oh dear, oh dear, oh, oh, now I've forgotten the name. I'll never dare show my face among my friends again.'

He looked with fear as he saw the animals approaching him. His heart beat fast, his whiskers trembled. 'It's no good, don't get excited and don't bully me, because I too have forgotten the name.'

The animals collapsed in heaps about him, some weeping, some sighing, some making no noise at all. 'Well, that's that,' they all said. 'No chance of survival now.'

'Please,' said a small voice, 'just let me have a turn.'

'Let you have a turn , what do you mean?'

'Let me go to the mountain spirit and ask the name of the tree.'

All the animals looked down and saw it was a tiny tortoise with a nice shiny shell on his back. 'You're such a slow walker; by the time you get back we'll be dead,' they said.

'I'll go as fast as I can,' said the tortoise. 'Please let me try?'

'Oh, oh, very well, off you go,' said the lion.

So the little tortoise turned and walked away slowly, slowly into the forest. Now the tortoise, although he was slow, was a very reliable creature. He plodded on and on, not setting himself too fast a pace so he would get tired, and not too slow in case he fell asleep. As he went he counted '37, 38, 39, 40,' each footstep he counted and by the time he got to the mountain spirit he had reached 29,563½.

'Oh, mountain spirit,' he said. 'I'm awfully sorry about this but I am afraid that the lion too forgot the name of the magic tree, so as a last resort, well I am rather slow, the animals have sent me.'

'I don't know what to think,' said the great mountain spirit. 'You're all very silly animals and if *you* don't remember the name I shan't tell it again. The name of the tree is Ewungelema – now go back to the forest and don't forget it.'

'Ewungelema,' said the tortoise, and he set off down the mountain side. 'Ewungelema, Ewungelema,' over the stones, over the grass, 'Ewungelema, Ewungelema,' over the dusty sandy soil 'Ewungelema, Ewungelema,' down to the dried up plants and bushes.

'Oh, what a large ant-hill. I think perhaps I'd better go around it, it's too large to climb. Ah! Here are the other animals. Ewungelema.'

'Well, well? Can you remember the name?'

'Ssh . . . wait till I get to the tree,' he called to them, muttering the name as he took the last few strides.

'Well, here's the tree, go on. What's the name?'

'EWUNGELEMA!'

The tree shuddered and shook, and from its branches fell juicy round fruit upon the heads of the animals. They ate and ate and ate their fill, and went to bed happy and content, their stomachs bursting with the juicy delicious food.

After that, they were able to eat each day from the tree until the famine was over. They were terribly pleased with the tortoise and never laughed about him being slow again. They almost made him King instead of the lion, but he was too modest to accept.

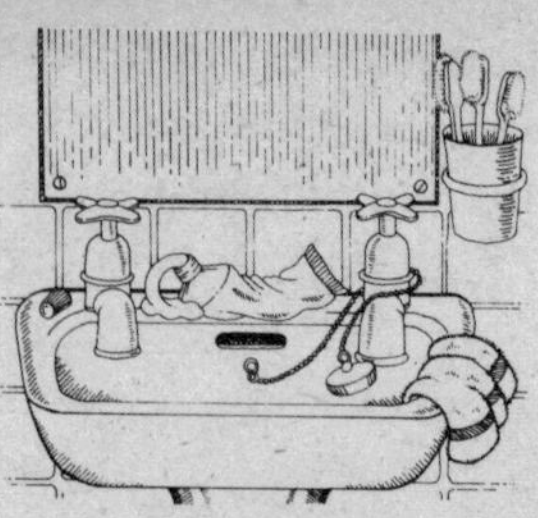

Freddie, the Toothbrush Cheat

Freddie sat at the kitchen table collecting crumbs and arranging them in a circle around the rim of his plate. His mother was at the sink, elbow deep in foam, washing the dishes after supper, and Freddie looked up at her feeling warm and full and sleepy. It would soon be bedtime; Freddie didn't mind going to bed too much in the winter when it was dark and cold outside and he could wriggle down in the bed with his comics and have a little read and a laugh before the light went out. But then his heart sank; he would have to have a bath and clean his teeth. Ugh.

Now Freddie was a jolly boy, who normally did as he was told, but he hated soap and water with all his heart. Even more he hated cleaning his teeth. The whole business bored and annoyed him so much that the thought of it made him want to hide from his mother, or even run away rather than have to go through with it again. He felt depressed and stuck his thumb in his mouth and gave it a good suck, at the same time twirling a strand or two of hair with the other hand. His mother had just finished putting away the last knife and fork in the drawer when she saw him from the corner of her eye.

'Come on Freddie, you look tired darling. It's half past six, I'll just go and run your bath.' And she went upstairs.

Freddie let out a groan and felt himself sag. 'Here we go again,' he thought. 'All that palaver. Soap in my eyes, up my nose,in my mouth and that awful, boring toothbrush.' He could bear it no longer and furtively climbed into the waste-bin and pulled the lid over himself. It was a bit smelly in there. There'd been kippers for tea and the bones crunched under his shoes but it was preferable he thought to the smell of rose-pink soap. He heard his mother re-enter the kitchen. She called him then sighed when he didn't answer. Lifting the flap of the waste-bin an inch or two he found himself gazing at her flowery apron and he quickly shut it again, but she heard the thud and pulled him out without ceremony and chased him up the stairs whacking his bottom with a loofah.

Freddie was in a frightful rage by now; he shouted and wailed, whilst his mother soaped and scrubbed him. The flannel got in his mouth, and his ears filled with bubbles, hot angry tears dripped into the lather as he slipped and slithered in an attempt to escape his mother's grasp, but she held him firmly and didn't let him escape until he was rosy and clean, and wrapped in a warm white towel.

'Oh, Freddie,' sighed his mother, rubbing his hair dry, 'I'm sick of you being so naughty at bath time; it really wears me out. You can clean your own teeth, I'm going downstairs to see if Daddy's home yet.'

Freddie sat on the bath room floor sucking his thumb. He was surrounded by little pools of water and patches of foam, the result of his battle. He hadn't won round one, but he was determined to win round two. He picked up his toothbrush, ran it under the tap, took the top off the tube, spread it here and there as if he'd spat it out in the bottom of the basin, and then got into bed feeling rather pleased with himself. He didn't know why but he didn't enjoy his comic that night; he couldn't smile once, not even at Korky the Cat who was usually his favourite.

The next morning, after breakfast, his mother said 'Go and clean your teeth, Freddie. I don't want to have to start the day with a quarrel so you can do them by yourself.'

Freddie climbed the stairs with a sly grin. He put his tooth brush under the tap, made a few splashing and spitting noises, spread a bit of toothpaste around the bottom of the basin and gazed triumphantly at himself in the mirror. He smiled gleefully, but quickly closed his mouth when he noticed that his teeth were not very clean.

For pudding that day, Mother had made blackberry pie and for supper they finished with chocolate mousse. Freddie was quite good in the bath that night and said he would clean his own teeth. After splashing the toothpaste around for a while he grinned in the mirror and was suprised to see his teeth were even dirtier with blackberry seeds stuck between them. He didn't sleep well at all.

The next morning after the same performance had gone on, Freddie bared his teeth and looked in the

mirror. He found to his dismay that the teeth were horrid. Still it was better than the boring business of teeth cleaning, and he was careful not to smile at anyone that day and only spoke with his hand over his mouth much to everyone's amazement.

That night he spent ages making teeth cleaning noises, spitting and sploshing about. He was afraid to look at his teeth which was hardly surprising for they were now quite disgusting.

The next few days were misery. He was afraid to speak, of course, and just answered his parents with a 'Mmmmm' or a nod. His mother didn't mention his teeth, but he couldn't help feeling he wished she would.

After four weeks of not cleaning his teeth, Freddie was a dreadful sight. And horror of horrors, his face ached. His mother, greatly distressed, took him to the doctor.

His examination was brief. 'This child has not been cleaning his teeth!' he said, 'He is suffering from toothache. There's nothing I can do for him I'm afraid. He'll have to go to the dentist!'

Freddie's mother was very cross. 'Why Freddie', she exclaimed, 'you are a silly boy. You think you've been cheating me but really you've been cheating yourself, and look what it's led to. I've never seen such a ghastly sight in my life. Put on your coat. We're off to the dentist at once'.

The dentist said. 'This is the worst case of non-teeth-cleaning I've ever come up against, my boy,' and he set to work.

Freddie was half an hour in the dentist's chair and his teeth were given a final polish with a tickly whizzing brush. Then the dentist handed him a mirror and said, 'Now smile Freddie – that's how your teeth should look'.

They were rows of gleaming white pearls set in firm pink gums – a lovely sight. Freddie's mother never had to tell him to clean his teeth again as you can well imagine. Nobody – not even Freddie – would rather have toothache than clean his teeth.

Books by **Enid Blyton** for younger readers.

The Boy Who Turned into an Engine	75p	☐
The Book of Naughty Children	85p	☐
A Second Book of Naughty Children	50p	☐
Ten-Minute Tales	75p	☐
Twenty-Minute Tales	85p	☐
More Twenty-Minute Tales	85p	☐
The Land of Far-Beyond	85p	☐
Billy-Bob Tales	50p	☐
Tales of Betsy May	75p	☐
Amelia Jane Again	60p	☐
Bimbo and Topsy	50p	☐
Eight O'Clock Tales	75p	☐
The Yellow Story Book	85p	☐
The Red Story Book	75p	☐
The Blue Story Book	75p	☐
The Green Story Book	75p	☐
Tricky the Goblin	50p	☐
The Adventures of Binkle and Flip	75p	☐
The Adventures of Mr Pink-Whistle	75p	☐
Mr Pink-Whistle Interferes	60p	☐
Mr Pink-Whistle's Party	60p	☐
Merry Mr Meddle	50p	☐
Mr Meddle's Muddles	60p	☐
Mr Meddle's Mischief	50p	☐
Don't Be Silly Mr Twiddle	60p	☐
Adventures of the Wishing Chair	75p	☐
More Adventures of the Wishing Chair	85p	☐

D281

A great selection of **Puzzle Books** from Granada.

Michael Holt		
Figure It Out 1	50p	☐
Figure It Out 2	50p	☐
Figure It Out 3	75p	☐
Figure It Out 4	75p	☐
Ronald Ridout		
Picture Words	75p	☐
Word Hunt	75p	☐
In Other Words	75p	☐
My Word	50p	☐
Word for Word	50p	☐
What's The Word	50p	☐
First Puzzles	50p	☐
Konky Puzzles	50p	☐
Active Puzzles	60p	☐
Puzzles Galore	75p	☐
More Puzzles	50p	☐
Top Puzzles	75p	☐
David Wells		
Solve It!	60p	☐
Roy Pickard		
Dragon Movie Quiz Book	75p	☐

Joke Books from Granada.

Cole/Thaler		
Knock Knocks	85p	☐
Thaler		
Funny Bones	50p	☐
Cole		
New Knock Knocks	80p	☐
Alan Jamieson		
Who Do You Know?	95p	☐

D481